Covington, KY

Back to the Light

Back to the Light

Poems

George Ella Lyon

UNIVERSITY PRESS OF KENTUCKY

Copyright © 2021 by The University Press of Kentucky

Scholarly publisher for the Commonwealth,
serving Bellarmine University, Berea College, Centre
College of Kentucky, Eastern Kentucky University,
The Filson Historical Society, Georgetown College,
Kentucky Historical Society, Kentucky State University,
Morehead State University, Murray State University,
Northern Kentucky University, Spalding University,
Transylvania University, University of Kentucky,
University of Louisville, and Western Kentucky University.
All rights reserved.

Editorial and Sales Offices: The University Press of Kentucky
663 South Limestone Street, Lexington, Kentucky 40508-4008
www.kentuckypress.com

Cataloging-in-Publication data is available from the Library of Congress.

ISBN 978-0-8131-8118-9 (hardcover : alk. paper)
ISBN 978-0-8131-8115-8 (pbk. : alk. paper)
ISBN 978-0-8131-8117-2 (epub)
ISBN 978-0-8131-8116-5 (pdf)

This book is printed on acid-free paper meeting
the requirements of the American National Standard
for Permanence in Paper for Printed Library Materials.

Manufactured in the United States of America.

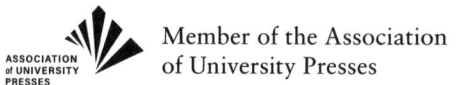

Member of the Association
of University Presses

In memory of Phyllis Jenness

"Sing with the voice you have,
not the voice you want."

Contents

Little Girl Who Knows Too Much   1

"One Way to Look at Your Life Is to Ask 'What Have I Done with My Breath?'"   5

Body Speaks   6

Out with It   8

Trapdoor   10

Debut   13

Wait, Weight   14

Thank You, Eric Andersen   15

Wings   17

About the Journey   21

She's   22

Pre-Parenthood   24

Receiving   26

Stuff   27

Pillow Talk   28

◎

The Great Mother Says *Growl*   33

Writer   34

Who and How   35

First Memory: Going to St. Ives   37

Stone Brought Home from the River Ouse   38

March 28, 1941   39

Fallingwater   40

◎

A Briefing   45

How Mean Poem Does   46

Meantime   47

An Exchange   48

Mean Temperature, or A Lesson by Degrees   49

Thirteen Ways of Looking at Mean Poem   50

◎

Fundamentals of Singing   57

Why I Fell at the Folger Shakespeare Library   61

Some Big Loud Woman   64

Mary   66

She Sings   69

◎

"Let Us Go Forth with Fear and Courage and Rage to Save the World"   73

Old Folk @ the Grocery   75

After the Wake   76

Possibilities   79

Breaking   80

Three Years On   81

Back to the Light   83

◎

Psalm   87

The Meadow Does Not Know   88

When   89

More   91

Bodywork   93

◎

World Tree   97

Acknowledgments   101

Notes   103

About the Author   105

Little Girl Who Knows Too Much

who in the third grade is savvy and wary
whose face is her grown-up face
who would welcome dullness but can't afford it
whose innocence has been slammed into insolence.
What happens at her house? Does she have
a house? Does she have a father, a brother,
a mother's lover who has forced on her
this face? She's in the front row. I can't help
but look at her. Even her clothes are uneasy.
She questions my spiel about writing as a way
to connect with your inside self, your story.
And where would that get me, old woman?
she seems to say. *I've still got to do a lot
of time as a child. I've got to try to save my
outside self, as you so stupidly call it. Go home
till you have something to say that helps.*

"One Way to Look at Your Life Is to Ask 'What Have I Done with My Breath?'"

—David Rubenstein

I held it
It went bad
I had it knocked out of me

I went in search of it
Under my shoulders
Above my belly
Behind my heart

It was wary
And held itself
Against me

I made promises:
I'll welcome the swell
Of the belly
I'll praise you
With open ribs

The breath sighed

I'll shout, I whispered
I'll ride your wave
With a song

Go look in your story
Breath said.
That's where you left me.

Body Speaks

Could I be the title?
I would like to be the title—
trade places with the head.
    ☺
You can't keep what's false
if you want what's true.
    ☺
To steel yourself
    is
to steal yourself.
    ☺
I will work with you.
            Will you?
    ☺
A skeleton
wearing
a suit
of armor:
what
a waste
of resources!
    ☺
You're like a head
with its chicken
cut off.
    ☺
Don't be afraid
at the bottom

of the breath.
There's more
where that
came from.
   ☺

If you won't listen to pleasure
I will have to speak pain.
   ☺

Trauma enters
unnamed places.

It cannot
get out
by itself.
   ☺

I
am with
you
through
thick
&
thin.
   ☺

Your parents
gave me to you
but now I'm all
yours.

Out with It

I'm telling you his name
was Fear Guilt Shame
I'm telling, I'm telling you
his name

I'm saying what he did
when I was just a kid
I'm saying, I'm saying
what he did

He took me in his room
maple bunk bed tomb
He took me, he took me
in his room

He was twelve and I was five
I left my body to survive
He was twelve, he was twelve
I was five

I told my mama and I cried
She turned stony, said I lied
I told my mama but she said
I lied

I was five and she was grown
so I made her truth my own

I was five and made her truth
my own

They were bigger than me
but I've labored to be free
Nothing's bigger, bigger
than free

So I'm telling you his name
was Fear Guilt Shame
He was twelve and I was five
And my mama said I lied

But they are gone I am grown
Now my truth is my own.

Trapdoor

Family Ford. Pennsylvania Turnpike.
She is—seven? eight? Supper
at Howard Johnson's, whose clam
strips and Boston baked beans
and many flavors of ice cream
are as exotic as India. Afterward,
before driving on, the family
walks up the parking lot hill
to what she will later understand
is an abandoned miniature golf course.

Dirty green carpet flapping,
windmill peeling. Seeing this ruin
of play, she almost remembers
the bunkbed and what
it took to be Princess for real.
A ground she didn't know
was there falls away. Inside she

is falling too. Hope hisses out
like air from a punctured lung.
What's wrong? her mother says.
Didn't we just have a perfect dinner?
Her daddy jingles his keys. Her brother
asks for baseball on the radio.
She pretends to perk up.

Debut

Dusty velvet maroon curtain. You
wait behind its pleated wall. Guitar
neck in your left hand, your best
friend's hand in your right. You're
fourteen, it's 1963, and the audience
creaks the wooden seats of your
high school auditorium, eager
to see the football queen crowned
and get back to the house. But they
must sweat through entertainment
first, including you and Joanie,
debuting your folk act, thanks
to "Lemon Tree" and "Blowin'
in the Wind." You're both trembling
like that windswept tree, breath
held till your names are called.
Then you step out into footlight's
dazzle, all hope and high hearts.
Somewhere in the universe your
voices still travel, a disturbance
of air, your first song.

Wait, Weight

Thursday, piano lesson day, I hadn't
practiced. I'm glad that's over, sitting
in the glider on Mrs. Welch's porch
waiting for my mother to pick me up,
not thinking about flats and naturals,
not thinking about andante and two-
against-three, but about it being
five-thirty and mother not there,
—I've been waiting a good half-hour—
and about how fat, fat, fat I suddenly
feel. Not my hands or feet, not
my ankles or calves, not my torso
from the waist up. No, it is
from my stalwart little waist to my knees.
This is heavy, this geography of sex,
amnesiac land where a boy I've never met
will fish for the future with his magic pole.
"Down there" my mother called it, like
it was someplace I couldn't even reach,
much less visit. "Through here"
was the region of breasts, not that she used
the word. When I got my first bra it was
because I was "developing." Fifty
years later I'm still waiting to see
the picture, still trying to welcome
that weight.

Thank You, Eric Andersen

I tore the thin vinyl disc
from my copy of *Sing Out!*
and dropped it down the spindle
of my 1965 gray and white stereo
set in a gold trolley with album rack
almost as big as a Smart car.
And out of that black disc
within a square
spun these words:

> *You've been sleepin' in the rain*
> *From the dirty words and muddy cells*

At sixteen, I had never been camping
much less tramping, much less in jail
but Eric Andersen's love song to the wronged
caught my heart. What in my well-fed,
dry-cleaned, leakless-roofed self found
a mirror in that song? Do we all have
an inner protester, out of doors, marching,
hungry, headed for bars, both liquored and iron?
Probably.   Also, a month before, I'd been
thrown out of my aunt's house on a snowy
day three hundred miles from home.
A small thing, relatively speaking. But
when I called my mother to explain, she

said she didn't know if she could believe
me. She didn't want to hear any more.
Ever. And Daddy must know nothing.
A cousin picked me up, drove me to
the bus. My parents met me. We rode
home in silence. For this, too, I wandered
the back roads of our house, looked out
the bars of my story. I needed that song.

Wings

> Say to your voice, "Go
> anywhere you want to.
> I won't stop you."
> —Phyllis Jenness

O, Voice, what if I'd let you go
to Greenwich Village as I dreamed?
What if you'd arrived, wearing
my sturdy little body in the fall
of 1967, who would have been there?

Richard Fariña was dead, Bob Dylan
in retreat, Odetta on tour. Lord knows
the whereabouts of Peter Paul and Mary.
Maybe you would have sung with Tom
Paxton: *And I can't help but wonder
where I'm bound, where I'm bound.*
Scared and lonely, you might have done it.

Or found a friend among classmates
at Columbia to sing with, someone who knew
more than your ten chords in first position.
You two would have sat up late in the dorm,
working out harmonies, writing new songs,
mapping laughter and rage in your hearts.

You would have dropped out, rather than
flunk out, and shared an apartment down

around 8th. It was cold. Hot water erratic
as your lyrics. And you had that gray
jeans jacket, remember? that you wore even
in snow because once, right after you sang
your latest song, the last of your set
at The Bitter End, and put on your jacket
to go, a total stranger came up and kissed
you between the shoulder blades.

About the Journey

I guess you thought you knew.
(I thought I knew.)
Surely we had a map.
(Who made the map?)
When you don't know where you're going,
isn't it better to go together?
Get acquainted along the way?
Discover each other
while you explore Lost?

If this is not sufficient, you
can produce, out of your bodies,
totally helpless creatures to help you along.
There's a purpose if you didn't have one.
There's a clue. Feed, bathe, change.
Keep vigil. Sort out who does what.

It's true, travel is harder with this crew,
but you don't know where you're headed,
so why rush to get there? Feed, bathe, change.
Isn't this wilderness lovely? Hold, sing, sleep.
You're having the time of your lives.

She's

six months gone
in a family way
out to here

She's showing

She's going to buy a baby
got one in the oven
bigged

She's knocked up

She's
expecting
eating for two
great with child

She's that
slight, round
teenage, menopausal
wonder

She's that
goldilocksed
kinky-headed
feather-braided
hidden-haired
girl

She's that
give-her-one-cell-
and-nine-months-
and-she'll-make-a-person

She's
that woman
who carried us
all

Pre-Parenthood

Though each of us has lived
a quarter of a century
we are babies
sitting in a borrowed bed
in our linoleum-floored bedroom
in our rented house
way out Elm Hill Pike
almost to the reservoir
sipping wine, crunching crackers.

I am reading myself onto
the Champs-Élysées in 1942
                      and Steve has landed on one
                      of Ursula Le Guin's imaginary planets.
Black-and-white newsreels
whirr in my head
and someone croons
"The Last Time I Saw Paris"
                      while in the furrowed field of Steve's brain
                      a baby sits in a patch of sunlight
                      which he pats with his plump palm
                      claiming it as "Mine sun,"
                      in Le Guin's *The Dispossessed*.

        In the meantime
        in the middle of me
           our son
           is rising
    he who in eight moons
will draw our worlds together

will hold out his arms
wider than the Boulevard Saint-Michel
and travel us
to a dimension we can't dream of
the one where we become
the ones, the two
who belong
to his breath.

Receiving

I had no idea how to hold a baby.
Forget instinct. It doesn't feel like it looks.
And you were a squirmer and wouldn't
stay swaddled. "Receiving blankets"
we called those cloths you threw off,
as though we'd held them
stretched beneath stars
while you fell from heaven.

In the yellow one with rabbits stamped on,
I wrapped you for our first trip out.
You wriggled and stretched and fought
with fists when I held you in the crook
of my arm. Laid on my shoulder, you
bellied around like a snake.

It was September. Hot. Hot.
And you smothered in a drawstring
gown and that blanket. I didn't have a grip.
That much was clear. And you were on
your journey, in search of something firmer
or freer. I still do not know which.

Stuff

is always pushing up out of the laundry basket, more, more, like a wound that won't heal. I believe there's a pocketbook at the bottom, but I don't know, I haven't seen it for years. Could be a hot water bottle, could be a little coping saw. You can't know unless you get down there, and I don't see that happening, what with days and clothes all piling up and up. Maybe it doesn't have a bottom anymore. Maybe it never did. Maybe there's a trapdoor through which the old ones push up the fabric of their lives for me to deal with: Papaw's work clothes, Papa Dave's khakis, Jo's delicates, Granny Buby's nightgowns. I expect the Greats have their garments in there, too, and that's why sometimes I'm scrubbing on a board, why I'm working by carbide light and then out in the yard with a washtub set up on sawhorses. Hog blood, chicken blood, birth blood. Keep going. Uniforms, bayonet-slashed and lice-infested. Their hands reach up out of the basket. I have to lock my knees and brace myself not to be pulled in, not to be drubbing moonrags free of blood in some ship's hold.

Pillow Talk

My life is too small, she says.
I need a bigger size
but I can't afford it.

It's your brain, he says.
That's what's too small.
Anyway, how much would it cost?

My body is too big, she says.
Too old too. I need a younger
smaller one. One of those strong
curvy ones with red hair.

I'd go for that, he says.

You want red hair?

No, I'd like you smaller, curvy.

Thanks a lot.

Don't be such a bitch.
I just want what you want.

You are not helping!
I'd like a heart with a verandah
open windows, white curtains blowing.
I'd like to welcome life, not be fear-locked.

I'd like to go to sleep, he says.

Go ahead, she says.
I'd like to wake up

The Great Mother Says *Growl*

What if your mother called you in and said, "You're in real trouble," only she was wearing the Virgin Mary's blue robe over her navy small-checked executive dress with the black leather belt thin as an eyebrow and she held an incense stick between her fingers instead of a Herbert Tareyton? What if she said, "Thank God! I thought you were never going to get in trouble. I've been really worried. But this is some good trouble at last."

And there you stand, perplexed and complexed, noticing all the flowers at her feet, wondering if this trouble has to do with the bird, till she puts one hand under your chin, tilts your face up, and says, "Show me your tongue."

So you stick it out, knowing she'll see where the bird scored that taste-speckled muscle with its beak.

"Ah ha!" she says. "Marked and strong. For tasting, kissing, speaking, singing. But it needs power. Growl."

"Growl?"

"Is something wrong with your ears? You heard me: growl."

"Grrrr."

"Did I say *purr*?"

"No."

"Let's hear it then."

"GRRRR—"

"Louder!"

"Grrrrrrr!"

"Deeper!"

"GRRRRRR!"

"Put your guts into it!!"

"GRRRRRRR!"

"Give it a hah! at the end."

"GRRRRRR-hah!"

"That's a start," she says. "Now grate this cabbage. We're having coleslaw for supper."

Writer

The page is not your limit.
This book, this room, they are not
your margins. You can write
on a street, a state, a continent.
You who wove your words out
of meadow grasses and hawk feathers,
write on the river. Write on the sky.
Write in between November sycamore
branches, on the line of a prairie
horizon. Write back to history.
Answer every note you ever received,
including those from birds. Ask your
dreams questions. Ask your body
for secrets. What words lodge
at the base of your spine
or under the heft of your breast?
Each stroke of your heart sends
rich red ink on its errands,
picking up food and air, brightening
speech. Think: You are never
inkless, always in the flow. You
have only to pick up a pen, small
wand that taps your great tree of life.
This is the season. You are
what you are.

Who and How

Emily was
a body
when she
wrote "I'm
nobody."

Now she is
no body
everybody
knows

The way the flower
takes the bee

and the bee
the flower

Her life was simple
at the beginning. She died
of complications.

Her father
her mother
her sister
her brother
her brother's wife
his lover

iron fence
white
room

Poems—
star-buds
in dark
of brick
and martyr

Galaxies
spiral
through
the soul's
keyhole

First Memory: Going to St. Ives

Playing in your mother's lap   fiddling with her beads
patting her soft arms, resting   your cheek against her breast.
See the red and purple flowers of her dress?   Hear the rattle
feel the rocking of the railcar   that carries you down Cornwall
to St. Ives? With your parents   six siblings and a cook, six servants
and a dog   You're going to fill your soul   with Talland House summer
awash in ocean   garden   light.

A pivotal mind,   an ovular voice   of literature in English
is tracing the curve of black beads   while we who read you now
are the unborn of the unborn of the unborn.   O ever expanding
universe we know not into what!   O Virginia, the roundness
of your cheek, the bounty   of your becoming!   By words
you will write almost sixty years on,   World War II darkening around you,
we take this train, touch those flowers,   travel the intricate track
you laid down.

Stone Brought Home from the River Ouse

Was the stone you slid into the pocket of your coat before you stepped into the river like the one I pulled from the water & carried in hand & suitcase & had to explain to the US customs inspector? "It's a rock," I told him. Chert: flint and chalk. What underlies Sussex, what underlay your life, what in the end pulled you under. "Just a rock?" he says, & I nod. "Looks like some sort of skull."

I think of how three weeks later, kids found your body, how all their lives they were the ones who saw what the river made of you. How perhaps one day they read your words, heard your voice ring out beyond all loss: mother, sister, father, brother, gone by your twenty-sixth year. The catastrophe of the First World War, the insanity of the Second. You

married to a Jew living on the coast Hitler all but had his foot on. Sky black with bombers, London, your soul's map, nightly obliterated. The world's madness brought yours back and so you walked into the river. You who wrote *Against you I will fling myself, unvanquished and unyielding, O Death!* Your words lift the stone from your pocket. See. I have it here.

March 28, 1941

What they remember
is your drowning

not your Olympic swimming
not those dives
those ecstatic surfacings

not how you caught
what flashed
beneath the billows

not how you wrote
on the waves.

Fallingwater

I fell at Fallingwater,
the most famous house
in America. I fell going to the waterfall.
I have a strong sense of metaphor, loved the house
set on a boulder, the boulder become a fireplace.
I placed fire at Fallingwater, a pain blaze
in my bone house, wedged
against another boulder at the floor
of the waterfall. I used my leg
as a lever, under the cantilever, to hold me up
and it did, and it bruised calf to shin,
knee to ankle. The house ledged over
the falls, its terraces all balanced
while I fell over the ledge, not art
just metaphor. Metaphorically speaking, I
fell, the great house stepped up behind me
"like gift boxes," the guide said, "balanced over
the edge of a table." Water table and it
falling
at Mill Run,
Pennsylvania.
Like my bank account,
my stamina,
my productive years. The Kaufmanns
are dead, who afforded and lived in
the house. Likewise Frank Lloyd Wright, who
designed it. Likewise stone masons
who laid walls

                                                    like ledges, concreters
                                                who poured
                                    a canopy
                                like a stream.
Chefs, maids, glassblowers, whoever filled the water pitchers,
    whoever built the literal fires that made the boulder bloom
                            All fell
                            like me
                                to gravity
                            at Fallingwater.
                        We build what we can't keep.
                    So I sat
                        tears sliding
                            over the ledge
                                of my eyelids.
                            I had to laugh.
                        It was Fall.
                    Fallingwater
                    fallingwriter
            I had fallen
                on the nature trail
                of a house trailing nature
            a house meant to be at home
                in this falling land   these woods.
                        The sign had said
                                At your own risk
                                    but that applies to everything
                                so I fell out of art
                                hard
                                    into my own flesh.

A Briefing

Mean Poem juices words
instead of mincing.
What are you making? I ask.
Meaning, she answers.

How Mean Poem Does

She stanzas around counting stresses
or puts her head down on the newel post
crying, *Essence!*
Mean, Mean, I say,
my hand on her shoulder
my other hand balancing the laundry,
What is it like?
Her face blazes up.
Are you saying
you would settle
for comparison,
take onion's word for dirt
and call it ground?
Know you not heart's horizon
wider than evening?
A path of light beyond
dead stars?

Meantime

Mean Poem stops by the house.
Winter. Five o'clock.
She's wearing jeans, a stray coat,
she's carrying an eggplant
and a bottle of wine.
I came to see what you've done, she says,
her breath rising in plumes.

In the kitchen I have to confess
I haven't written.
I wash the eggplant, pour the wine,
define the weight
of two new jobs.
Mean stares
as though I fell out of the sky.

And if they were hiring a tree
would you apply? I know
you can look like a tree.
And a cornfield.
You don't fool me.
Nobody in her right brain
meaning to write
would keep this up.
Or do you reckon
on getting a second life?
We all have to trot out
and do things for money
but if you think a wage
is a living
I give up.

An Exchange

A week and no word
from Mean Poem. She doesn't
have a phone, so I go
to her house. I keep a key.

Now Mean doesn't read books—
she moves into them.
Among wrinkled sheets, amid
covers and spines
for the longest time, she doesn't
know I've come.
Then at a break, she returns.

I was going to fix us
some lunch, I say,
but there isn't any food.
Mean, you've got to get up
and go to the grocery.
I'm at the grocery, she answers.
And look here, you're almost
out of wood. She waves
a book titled *Fire*.
Be serious, Mean. When you're
empty and cold, you'll wish
you'd thought of these things.
Funny, she says. *That's
my advice to you.*

Mean Temperature
or A Lesson by Degrees

It was one of those days—
guilt on the kitchen stove,
guilt in the laundry basket.
I had done everything wrong
in order to write.
No board game with the children.
No steaming face above smiling soup.
Mean, I said, you see how this is:
to succeed in one place, I fail
in another. I can't hold
someone's hand and a pen.

I do indeed, said Mean.
You sound sick. She put
her tough hand on my forehead.
Yes. Two degrees. Or is it three?
How many degrees have you got?
And where from? Are you the glue
that holds the world together?
Air that all your loved ones
must breathe? Don't be indispensable
if you don't want to be a dispenser.
Love can wear the same socks twice.
And love, old enough, can wash its own socks.
You make the poem come clean.

Thirteen Ways of Looking at Mean Poem

    1
Look again.

    2
Is it her feathers
that shine
as she perches
on the gutter
or the song
with which she preens
her wings?

    3
By kelp and calyx
by stamen and stamina
words nourish the mute
body of the world.
By digit and phalanx
by palm and thumb stump
they give the grave beast
hands.

    4
She's lazy
self-indulgent
a poor citizen.
Words to her
are more real
than money.
Her hem sags
her cupboard sags
there are bags

under her eyes
and all over
her house.
Everything she keeps
and gives away.
She takes in strays
she can't afford to feed
and then expects
to make ends meet
with metaphor.

    5

She doesn't always write
on the lines
the subject
or the paper.
She may produce
paper-plate poems,
rhymes on a bus-ticket folder.
She isn't even neat
about her work.
She's not responsible.
It's not territory, she says.
I don't own it.
I don't own
but shape
what comes to me sometimes.
Of course it shapes me too
like the potter who finds
her face is a bowl
her belly a platter

her hands shallow dishes.
Other times
the poem roars through
like an express train
not stopping at the station
and my vaults shake
my chandeliers sway
my whole construction
hums.

6
No wonder
she doesn't have
any money.

7
She is afraid
of the telephone
and angry
at the telephone
and doesn't have
a telephone
and loves to talk.

8
Things she brings with her:
a dingy oriental rug
a rattan fan chair
two cats, a dog
a suitcase that's more words
than clothes.

9
Do visions count?
May I tell you
about my vision
of Mean Poem
though it happened
in a dream?
How the night sky
became a TV screen
and the rearrangement of stars
announced her death?

10
This was a dream too.
Mean Poem was recognized
celebrated like an astronaut
in the streets of a major city.
She was the eye
of a parade
snaking through those streets.
Like a politician, a beauty queen
she sat in the back
of a convertible
and smiled at the falling
flowers, the showers
of confetti.
When the car reached

the platform
built and festooned
for her reading

the crowd rushed forward
lifted her out
and there, swelling
with shouts and song,
they ate her.

    11
Mean Poem is asleep.
The soles of her feet
are caked with dirt.
There are tulips
in a jelly jar
on the table.
There is ink
on her tongue.

    12
Flight
and breath
fire
and song
blackbird
gives us
air.

    13
Give up
give in
give out
give over
        to love
        to the love
        of words.

Fundamentals of Singing

To sing, the teacher says,
you must breathe
and relax your jaw.

But there's a boy's hand
clamped over her mouth
as he does what he did
when she was five

and like another
hand, her mother's
words strike—
> You
>   make
>   things
>   up

Loosen the tongue, the teacher says,
to free the voice.

At thirteen
after stammering
attempts to tell
truth
she can't remember
she tries to leave
this life

Driving around afterward
her mother says
"This will kill your father

if he finds out. You must
never speak of it again.
Next year, you'll change
schools. Tonight you'll
start dance class."

Stretch and bend, shake out tension.
Your whole body is your instrument.

She is fourteen
when the phone rings
one fall morning
before school
and her aunt's voice
vibrates into
her mother:

"My daughter tried
to kill herself. She's in
St. Elizabeth's and it's
your daughter's fault.
I've read her letters—
dramatic, dangerous."

A complete breath
is the foundation of singing.
Let the air fill your torso.

After the call
she tells her mother

"I was just trying to help!"
"That makes it worse,"
her mother says. "You
don't know your own
intentions. This could
break up the family.
Do you hear me?
You will never speak
or write to your cousin
again. And watch yourself
with other people too."

Relax the throat, the teacher says.
Let the voice flow with no restriction.

She is trying
to sing through
rags of words
stuffed in her mouth
scars of words
rigid as a bit.

She is telling her tongue
you are not a sword,
saying to her breath
you speak true.

Every note
undoes
a knot

in self
and song.

Every breath
gives back
the right
to be.

Why I Fell at the Folger Shakespeare Library

For decades I've told the story:
how, impressed with myself,
I bought foolish shoes
for a big reading in D.C.
How I tossed aside my rule—
Never Wear Shoes You Can't
Run In—for bone-beige leather-
and-suede slightly heeled pumps.

I've said that's why I fell
on the intricate parquet stage
freeing poems to fly
and requiring me
on hands and knees

        to grope

                for

"Salvation"

                "Her Words"

                              "The Bowl"

      "Stripped"

        before standing
     to make my way
to the podium.

I've laughed at my first line:

At least that's over

and mocked my distress
as I peered into dark
and saw my parents had come.
Nine hours they'd driven
from Kentucky
only to witness the sprawl
of an awkward daughter's pride.

Then, at the reception,
a family friend from my hometown
came from behind, turned me,
and kissed me on the cheek.
"I'm living in Fairfax now," he said.
"Sorry I was late and stumbled in."

"*You* stumbled?" I said, choking
on pinot noir. My mother gave
him a hug. I told the story:
my downfall, my vanity,
those shoes.

The century would be gone
before my mind knew
what this neighbor had begun
when he was twelve
and I was five:
          how, his hand

over my mouth, he'd
forced me down. How
he'd split my life. Nobody
will believe you, he'd said
and he was right.

Who was I kidding
disguised as a poet
claiming that I had a voice

Just his approach
homing in on the Folger
would fling me to the floor
tear words from my hands
have me groveling

right where he'd left me.

Some Big Loud Woman

I need to listen to some big loud woman
                Orangey red
    Wild-haired
Her voice like
                A waterfall of kettles
Her head back   eyes shut
    Back arched
To roar that music out

I need the brass and bramble
    Of her low notes
The trembling windows
    Of her high

Bare feet planted on the floorboards
Green dress a summer canopy

The wail in one line
A scar on the air

I need to listen to a big loud woman
Heavy fists
    Pounding my table
Her anger
    Fire in the hearth

I need the avalanche

     Of her laughter
  The flood
     Of her truth

I need to listen
  To some big loud woman

I need some big loud woman to listen to

Mary

—for Mary Travers

When you were young
and lanky, graceful
bones visible, your wide
mouth and bright hair
made a vivid frame
for your voice.
On either side of you
dark-suited men
played guitars and sang
their fingers dancing.

Your instrument
was that body.
A woman, you carried
the melody or high harmony
the descant, or low
weave of thirds and fifths
and beauty too.
You had to be beacon
virgin, siren
little girl and vamp.
It comes to us at birth
this mantle—
No way to step onstage
without reference to it.

So you worked it,
shaking your hair

like a flag in the wind.
You were an actress after all.
No use to wear the mantle
like some ratty carpet remnant
when you could perfect
that dazzling twirl
managers, photographers,
and audiences swooned for.
It wasn't just the erotic
kick you bore like any
torch singer, but the shiny
energy advertising tomorrow
that rides a young woman's flesh.

In fact, you were already
a mother, your daughter
mostly out of view. A grand-
mother, now—heavy, clear
lines gone—you've survived
back surgeries, leukemia, bone
marrow transplant. Peter
and Paul, gray, thick, and bald
betray nothing. But you!
Some folks can't hear you
now because of what they
see, since your look was your
sound was your message round
and round the spindle
of image and desire.

Yes, your voice is lower, brassier
but Peter's and Paul's have
grown raspy, too, yet no website
bears their distorted pictures
like ones of you I found captioned
"Repulsive" and "Jabba the Hutt."
And you the same woman who helped
rally the "I Have a Dream" march,
who with mother and daughter
went to jail for protesting apartheid,
who gave your voice to changing
the times, to turning a nation.

These days you come onstage
with a cane and sparse wavy
after-chemo hair, bearing another
torch for us, the light of believing
anyway and laughing, the wise
slow steps of carrying it on.

She Sings
      —thanks to *How to Suppress Women's Writing*
      by Joanna Russ

She sings but she sings the wrong song.
She sings but she sings the song wrong.
She sings but it's not a real song.
She sings but she should be ashamed.
She sings but you don't want to hear it.
She's not really singing.
Someone else is working her mouth.

She sings but it's too soft to hear.
She sings but it's too loud to listen.
She sings but she swallows the words.
She sings but she belts it out.
She sings but look where she does it.

She sings but o my God that accent.
She sings but did you see her teeth.
She sings but look at those clothes.
She sings but where are her children.
She sings but you know about her mother.
She sings but she stole that song.
It's not just her mouth she opens.

She sings but she has no rhythm.
She sings but her playing is terrible
her house is a wreck
she doesn't have a man.

She sings but her man is a woman.
She sings when it's not time for singing.
She sings when we told her not to.
We told her we want quiet.

We told her to shut up.
We showed her the gag.
She keeps singing.

"Let Us Go Forth with Fear and Courage and Rage to Save the World."
—Grace Paley

It can't be done, I know, so don't start.
But didn't Grace go to Vietnam
to bring prisoners home?
Didn't she get arrested at the Pentagon?
Spend a month in Women's Detention
for sitting down in front of a tank
and holding up a flower?
Didn't she march against Nixon?

More than forty years later,
it's War Without End, Amen.
But Washington Park was saved
from Robert Moses' plans
to extend 5th Avenue through it.
And New York lost its bid
to ban music from the Park.
Disgraced and broken, Nixon
left the White House
and those POWs did come home.

Like her socialist parents, imprisoned
in Russia, then freed when the czar had a son,
Grace knew that the world can't be saved
but history can be changed
if enough truth is told
by people who get in the way.

So she stood
on a New York City street corner
wearing a sign that said
>   MONEY
>   ARMS
>   WAR
>   PROFIT
>   WALL STREET

She calls us now
to move through our fear,
muscle our courage,
and give rage a voice.

Old Folk @ the Grocery

I thought I saw Mary Travers at the Beaumont Kroger—
Mary in her middle years: ample. Jangled, I reached for
walnuts instead of apples. I have seen, via Wi-Fi, Mary's
grave. I watched, via YouTube, her memorial. I'm wary
of my heart's readiness to behold her alive, thirty
years younger, in a supermarket in the state where
she was born. Re-seen, after reckoning, this grocery
Mary is a far cry from that blond with the famous voice
heard here every Thursday during oldies' discount day.
"The answer is blowin' in the wind" she gives us, as we
navigate the produce aisle. Later, in dairy, "And when I
die . . . there'll be one child born and a world to carry on."

After the Wake
—for Josephine Catron Carson

Now that you have crossed that river
now that we have sung you
to the other side
have taken leave
of your service and feast
your ashes
your house

Now that it is all behind us
and you far beyond us
what do we have
but your words
planted in the bygone dirt of your days
words that are still, by Dog,
climbing the trellis
of this unparalleled
(yes, I know) moment
and blooming like the Dickens
and the Welty bloom
against the always-turning pages
of their skies

Oh, Jo, I am trying to say
the unsayable again
because, after all, it's my
rich and unpaying job—
same one you showed up for
at the door of every blessed day

Lift the lid on the brain-pot
stir up the heart-fire
and see what's cooking

I realize I've traipsed in
from garden to kitchen
wordwise, but so did you,
Bear following close

Unceasingly at your wake
that old black dog
searched for you
among mourners eating
cheese dip in your kitchen-
dining-living-dying room,
playing ukuleles and stand-up
bass by the firepit in your yard,
talking, singing their grief.
Bear beseeched each guest
to *be* you or, failing that,
to *bring* you or, failing that,
to take her somehow *to* you.
She could not rest.

We had each other—
distraction, consolation,
Spirit-drinking and conjuring.
No one wanted to leave
and take your absence

with them. But we did, Jo,
saying goodbye to your dying
in that red-spread bed, in that
cinder-block nest with your
Day-of-the-Dead walker
foursquare in the corner,
with your walking stick/
mage's staff collection hung
like the rungs of a ladder
on the wall

Now I want to make
a dazzling finish—
to say how at last
your ever-reaching spirit
has climbed another ladder
breathless
to the next world

but you say, "That's bullshit,
George. It's pretty, and pretty
ain't what it took to get me
out of my body, out of that
house, and all that held me.
Say what I said: 'We are
by design supposed
to let go the hard stuff
and live in love.'"

Possibilities

It's so so windy. I'm going to go take a walk
around the pond, maybe across the road,
past the cul-de-sac, up the wooden steps
onto the boardwalk and thus to the beach.

Around the pond, maybe across the road
I might see the living-green gold-banded stripe
that yesterday slithered from asphalt onto grass

Past the cul-de-sac, up the wooden steps
I might meet my older self, white-haired, helped
by two daughters and a three-pronged cane

onto the boardwalk and thus to the beach
or maybe my own mother, borne back from
the other side of time's waves breaking forever.

Breaking

Two years ago today my mother died,
eighty-nine and brilliant, stubborn, brave.
I broke one of her cardinal rules and cried

aloud in the hospital hall—alive, beside
myself with all she took and all she gave.
Two years ago today my mother died.

Three weeks before, she'd been at work, pride
for a moment stronger than death's wave.
I broke one of her cardinal rules and cried—

a lost daughter, the child she said had lied
as if that would keep a monster in its cave.
Two years ago today my mother died

and freed us from her rules, where shut inside,
we'd buried joy and anguish to behave.
I broke one of her cardinal rules and cried

made a scene, a spectacle, did not hide
my grief that it was me now I must save.
Two years ago today my mother died.
I broke the rules, I found love's voice. I cried.

Three Years On

I drop a white plastic bag
that holds

> Christmas sweater
> pink shirts
> nightgown
> and the brown and gold outfit
> you wore on your eighty-eighth birthday

into the Gaia charity box
by the world's last video store.

I bless you on your way, my mother
who all my life have been

> heart of my heart
> though your hurt
> turned my heart
> for a time
> against me

Scars kept you
from opening your arms
I reach high
to break adhesions

as I lift the last batch
of your raiment
        with one hand
pull down the yellow
metal door
        with the other

Back to the Light

When the men with the hammers had gone
the house was gone too. So I climbed down
the tree and just kept climbing, through
the ground into the kingdom of roots. Some
red thing called me. I crawled down a live brown
tunnel, then reached a place where I could stand.

A rise in the root path, a turning, and a little girl
in a red coat stood facing away. I came close,
saw the brown high-top shoes, the dark, bobbed hair,
the black velvet collar it barely grazed. "Hey," I said,
"How did you get here?" but she didn't answer.
Her shoulders were square and she stood tall. If she
was lost, she had another word for it. I touched
her arm. She didn't turn. The only movement
was the rise of her shoulders with her breath.
I walked around in front of her and knelt,
saw three velvet-covered buttons clasp
the coat at her breast. She was my mother.

"Let's go home," I said. She shook her head.
"Preshie left me here. Lane will come to get me."
Preshie was the hired girl, Lane her oldest brother.
"He sent me," I said. Her face lightened a little.
"On Old Gray?" "No. You know how horses are.
He wouldn't come down here." "Spooked," she said.
"That's right. So come back with me." "Are you
reliable?" she asked. I pondered that.

I'd been singing in a tree while workmen
unhammered my house. Still I said, "Yes."
Surely sun and air with me would be better
than waiting among roots. No one was coming
back. All long dead: parents, brothers, sisters,
Preshie, my father. My brother wouldn't come.
His house would never be unhammered
nor would he climb above or below ground.
But a little girl had been trapped there.
And now she walks with me back to the light.

Psalm

The Earth is my Mother.
I shall not want.
She invites me to lie down
in green pastures.
She offers me the calm
of still waters.
She restores my soul.
She leads me in the paths
of right relationship
for our home's sake.

Yea, though I walk
in the circle of life and death
I shall fear no evil
for I belong here.
Goldenrod and walking staff
they comfort me.
She prepares a garden before me
in the presence of my emptiness.
My cup is full.
Surely wholeness and mystery
shall follow me
all the days of my life
and I shall dwell
in Earth's sweet fields
forever.

The Meadow Does Not Know

about the stock market.
Today she is worth
exactly what she was worth
yesterday, a year ago, at creation.
I don't mean property value,
taxable assets. I mean
milkweed and copper moths
honeybees, cow vetch,
king snakes. Meadow life
is not money. What rises
and falls here are stems
and flowers, leaves and fruit.
No zigzag line of profit and panic
but the great wheel turning.
Here God gives of her
extravagance and here, like
flicker, viceroy, dragonfly
we come into our inheritance.

When

When I think of that beach
when I think of where the planes landed
when I was a Barra boy
when I think back generations
before the planes
when I ran, a little girl with braids flying
down the strand from my Ma to my Da
when I remember being the Da
hoisting my boy to my shoulders
walking home in twilight
sky the color of doves
when I remember being the Ma
stirring fish-head stew
in the iron pot over the fire
when I remember changing the straw
in our pallets, dreaming of a feather tick

I can see blisters on my least one's arm
when she bumped my hand
as I ladled up dinner
I see her feet
in the straw shoes my Ma plaited

and I am young again
wild as a girl
feisty as a boy
a man tall in his strength

a woman full in her giving
and the light of this earth
shines through me
and time is the way
we join hands

More

God arrived in a gypsy wagon

She came up the subway steps

She was so tired after work
that we ate cheese and radishes for supper
laughing into twilight
pollen on our shoulders

God came to my desk
She asked if I knew
how to get out of the way
While I was rooting around for an answer
she drank my coffee.
I like it cold, she said.

When I entered the house
of my dying friend
my ribs bound in fear
God was already there
sitting on the edge of the bed.
She scooted over.
I kissed my friend who asked
What do you know about
the limbic brain? She was
writing about this when cancer's
tide rolled in. This time
it was carrying her out. God

put Her arms around us.
Her wings.

God gave me Her hand
and it was more
than I could hold.

Bodywork

Through parted curtains of muscle on my back, I enter a long-ago home. Old woman/witch/my mother orders me to go down into the cellar and bring up food. I do, but the jar holds a fetus in a bloody broth. The woman yells at me and smashes the jar against the ground. "Go back!" I do, with the same result. "Go again!" she orders. I try to get away. She beats me with her walking stick, so I go. All the jars are ripe with dead babies. I come up and tell her this. She rages. I grab her stick and hit her, and with her black-gone-green coat flapping, she rises into the air and joins a flock of vultures.

From my tight back to my out-of-kilter hip, the healer's hands move. And from behind that bone ache, my just-dead friend comes zooming out, riding on a star. "You're gonna love this!" Jo says, and my heart lifts.

The healer's hands move again. I don't want to go back to the old woman's field. I try to steer my consciousness some other way, but there is none. I am there. It's Ireland. Ironland. Now there is no old mother/witch to tell me what I must do, but it could not be clearer. No, No, I say, as I pull the cottage off its foundation and throw it to the side like a tarp. No, No, as I return to the cellar to gather the jars in my arms, carry them up, smash them, carry up more, smash those too, till all are gone. Black wings swoop down, hungry beaks devour the pink-white forms. Light dances up from each stopped life. The babies are free. Where I flung the tarp, a new cottage rises, but I don't go in. My work here is done.

World Tree

1

Cornered by myself
at the living room desk
I'm eating chamomile flowers
from a plastic bag.
Over my shoulder
my husband's at the door
about to take our small son
to the park. "I cannot be
this way," I tell him.
"I cannot bear it."

2

In the dining room
I turn to the hall
expecting to pass
between bookcase and closet
and almost collide with

                older than everything
                furrowed like hickory
                smooth as beech
                sycamore dappled
                an enormous tree
                has split the floor
                pierced the ceiling
                thrusting up through
                the second story

out the roof
on to forever

Gray-brown bark
thunderous branches
rooms built among them
wounds patched with tin
shake my heart like a rattle
"Mother!" I scream
then call out, "Steve!"
knowing he won't hear
sure that he's gone
but he yells through the door
"Take a pill! Take a pill!"

3

A maroon haze
veils the living room
and I see through
the shut front door
a line of souls
streaming toward me
in armor
and nightdress
in buckskin
and sari
in ermine
in rags

on and on
they flow through me
as I stand
open
like the roof
my feet sending roots
far below the house
my arms lifted

Acknowledgments

The author wishes to thank the editors of the following publications or presses where versions of these poems have appeared:

From George Ella Lyon, *She Let Herself Go: Poems* (LSU Press, 2012), "Receiving," "Some Big Loud Woman."
English Journal, "Writer."
Earth Poems, "The Meadow Does Not Know."
The Oxford American, "Breaking."
Larkspur Press, "Psalm."
Shenandoah, "Who and How."
Limestone, "Wait, Weight."
Still: The Journal, "Old Folk @ the Grocery," "Why I Fell at the Folger Shakespeare Library," "World Tree" (as "Yggdrasil").
New Works Review Online, "Fallingwater."
Appalachian Heritage, "When," "March 28, 1941."
The Louisville Review, "Possibilities."
Sow's Ear, "The Mean Poems."
Motif 4: Music, "Mary."
Jocarson.net, "After the Wake."

Thank you to dear friends and poem workers Diane Gilliam, Marie Bradby, Martha Gehringer, Leatha Kendrick, Janece Walters-Cook, Louise Borden, Ann W. Olson, Sue Churchill, Sherry Chandler, Bruce Florence, Rebecca Gayle Howell, Nikky Finney, and Katerina Stoykova.

Thank you to healers Barbara Bauman, Karen DiGirolomo, Dinah Blue, Jutta Kausch, and Ann Boone

and to teachers Dick Jackson and Jeremie Leckron, to everyone at the University Press of Kentucky, especially Patrick O'Dowd, Ila McEntire, and Jewell Boyd

and to my husband Steve, whose love, vision, and humor make it all possible.

Notes

I met Phyllis Jenness (1922–2020) on the corner of Main and Broadway (or "prayer and sirens," as we called it), where we stood as part of the Interfaith Prayer Vigil for Peace after 9/11. A retired professor of vocal music at the University of Kentucky and founder and former director of the Lexington Singers, Phyllis was teaching "Be a Better Singer" classes and donating the tuition to charity. I signed up. Her teaching and her friendship changed my life. I'm sure many of her students would say the same.

"Debut": The songs mentioned are Bob Dylan's "Blowin' in the Wind" from *The Freewheelin' Bob Dylan* (1963) and Will Holt's "Lemon Tree," made popular by Peter, Paul and Mary on their eponymous debut album (1962).

"Thank You, Eric Andersen": The lyrics quoted are from "Thirsty Boots," which was included on his 1966 album *'Bout Changes 'n' Things*.

"Wings": The lyrics here are from Tom Paxton's "I Can't Help But Wonder Where I'm Bound," released on *Ramblin' Boy* (1964).

"She's" is dedicated to my daughter-in-law Whitney Gore.

"Stone Brought Home from the River Ouse": "Against you I will fling myself, unvanquished and unyielding, O Death!" comes from Woolf's novel *The Waves* and is carved on the plaque that marks her grave in the Monks House garden.

"Mary" honors Mary Travers (1936–2009), singer and activist. With bandmates Peter Yarrow and Noel Paul Stookey, she sang at the 1963 March on Washington, the Selma-Montgomery March, and many other demonstrations for peace and for social and environmental justice.

"Let Us Go Forth with Fear and Courage and Rage to Save the World" calls on the witness of writer and activist Grace Paley (1922–2007), whose commitment to feminism, community, and peace shaped her life and shines through her fiction and poetry in such collections as *Long Walks and Intimate Talks* and *Enormous Changes at the Last Minute*.

"Old Folk @ the Grocery": The song quoted at the end of this poem is Laura Nyro's "And When I Die," featured on *More Than a New Discovery* (1967).

"After the Wake" is dedicated to Jo Carson, "my sister or the same as." Poet, playwright, fiction writer, actor, and activist, Carson wrote out of her love for her place—Johnson City, Tennessee—and her people. Like Grace Paley, she listened for the personal and political truth in everyday voices in such books as *Stories I Ain't Told Nobody Yet* and *The Last of the Waltz Across Texas*.

"When": Barra is an island in the Outer Hebrides off the coast of Scotland.

About the Author

GEORGE ELLA LYON, former poet laureate of Kentucky, is the author of ten collections, most recently *She Let Herself Go, Many-Storied House*, and *Voices of Justice*. Her poem "Where I'm From" has gone around the world as a writing model. Lyon works as a freelance writer and teacher and lives in Lexington.